Cull of April

*"Au fin parler de France:
un très humble et passionné servant."*
– F. V.-G.[1]

I0560131

Francis Vielé-Griffin

Translated by Richard Robinson

---

[1] *"Au fin... servant"*: French for "To the end, speaking of France: A very humble and passionate servant." – F. V.-G.

Sunny Lou Publishing Company
Portland, Oregon, USA
http://www.sunnyloupublishing.com

2nd Edition, Corrected and Revised: December 3, 2025
2nd Edition: February 14, 2024
Original Publication Date: November 22, 2021

Translation Copyright © 2021 Richard Robinson.
All rights reserved.

ISBN: 978-1-955392-57-0

* * *

This translation from French is based on the
Société du Mercure de France's first edition of
Poèmes et Poésies, Paris, 1895.

Contents

Foreword

One month ago, I had never heard of Francis Vielé-Griffin before, at least I did not think I had, until someone had brought him to my attention.

Anyone can look up Francis Vielé-Griffin's details online or in book to discover more about this excellent poet – I would recommend the *Encyclopædia Britannica* (http://www.brittanica.com) to begin with. An American by birth, and born in Virginia in 1864, Griffin moved to France when he was seven or eight years old and "remained there for the rest of his life." His first book of poetry, the one in your hands, "showed influence of the Decadent movement."

That was my brief introduction to him, before having read any of his work. But then it donned on me that maybe, just maybe, I had run across his name before. And I knew just where to look. I took out a copy of Émile Goudeau's excellent who's who of artists and poets from the Belle Epoque, – *Ten Years a Bohemian* – sure enough, I found his name there, in chapter 12. And I quote:

> Others as well debuted, on one or another of those *chariots of Thespis*: there was d'Esparbès, Jean Ajalbert, Darzens. Other young men such as René Ghill, F. V. Griffin, Henri de Régnier, Morice got together in groups in the Latin Quarter, far from the Moulins de la Galette, near the old sacred Pantheon and noble Odeon; a new journal was founded, *Lutèce*. Georges Rall and Léo Trézenick improvised as printers, compositors even, page layout artists, correctors, to create with their hands that collection. They were a little aggressive against old comrades more or less "arrived" and, either by conviction or out of spite for competitors, they went and rediscovered Paul Verlaine, whom unjust fate had buried alive, and shined a light on Stéphane Mallarmé, who had no more need for it, it was felt, than, for example, the forgotten Raimbaud [sic]. Whatever! Since then, new leaders were found,

not personalist leaders who said to everyone: Do as
you like, provided you do it well! No, but the recon-
stitution of schools and coteries. The newcomers ral-
lied around master Verlaine, or chief Mallarmé, and
from there came the *Decadents* (of which the *Deli-
quescents* are nothing but parodists), the *Symbolists*,
and the *Instrumentalists*. The very amusing parody by
Adoré Floupette (Henry Beauclair and the poet
Gabriel Vicaire), the small opuscule entitled *Deli-
quescences*, was noticed by Paul Arène, who spoke
for a long time about it in *Gil Blas*. That made the
young decadents known. In the period of Roman
decadence, there were lesser poets, *poetæ minores*,
who used and abused rhythms, alliterations, plays on
words, convolutions, like Claudian, for example.
Some Parnassian poets, holding them in high esteem,
compared themselves to them. What's more, the word
decadent implies, beyond affectation of style, a cer-
tain disorder fundamentally, a hybrid blend of old re-
ligions and refined mores; that was also what the
decadents strived for; a particular sadism where
Catholic incense is detected in loathsome places, and
where the sanctuary has foul smells of face powder or
even washbasin water.

It's a longer quote than needed if only to show mention of his name;
its alternate purpose is to situate him in time, in milieu, among con-
temporaries, the artists whom this excellent American-French poet
rubbed shoulders with in or after the 1880s. One imagines him at the
Hydropaths Club sometimes. One notices the word decadence.

#

Whether Griffin was a Decadent poet, or a Symbolist poet, or even a
Romantic poet is probably not all that important, in the end, to the
ten or twelve readers today who might discover him in English (or
French even). Students of French literature in undergraduate or grad-
uate programs at university may find the literary categorizations im-
portant and useful, yardsticks by which to evaluate artists' works, to
understand them in a larger context of common themes and inten-

tions, and to write about them more easily, to learn about them in neat packages; literary categorizations also make it easy for publishers to target dilettantes and literary epicures of particular genres, to turn a greater (if any) profit thereby or to try to. But for the readers, such as myself, who don't read much literature from artists who cut their teeth after 1950, the year of founding of that egregious modern movement of poetry called Beat Poetry (with the rare exception of Gary Snyder) – inaugurating, from that moment forward, the great decline and true decadence of poetry to such low levels and abysses as street poetry or rapped poetry, poetry of the masses for the masses, poetry from the sewer, and Pulitzer-prize winning poetry of the last 5 or 10 years if not earlier – the classifications only matter in order to inform a person what *not to read*; but flippant (half-serious) atrabiliousness aside, ultimately a poet or an artist will be excellent, rotten, or something in between, regardless of what school someone says he belongs to.

In this his first book of poetry, *Cull of April*, Griffin's style and subject matter suggest influences of and possibly on (in my mind at any rate) – various artists whose verse I'm familiar with, *viz.* Jules La-Forgue, Auguste Villiers de l'Isle-Adam, Wallace Stevens, and Émile Goudeau. Sometimes there are hints of Paul Verlaine even, but mostly from *Cellulely*, and that's only when Verlaine is imitating someone else, say Villiers or Coppée. Apparently there is also a strong influence in this book of poetry of (not on) Stéphane Mallarmé.

Here is an example, from poem VII of "Euphonies," of a couplet that I particularly like and that suggests to me something of the style of Wallace Stevens:

> *I ramble on return from vain lassitudes,*
> *Have we not dreamt of other beatitudes?*

Can you hear the influence on? Can, can't, maybe? It does not matter. What matters most is that it is excellent.

– Richard Robinson, November 21, 2021.

Dedication

Here are the old sweet verses, our childish pride,
All your joy, credulous, alert, and mine;
How loud they were sung, how early in the morning,
How little we feared that maturity would arrive!

It came without a sound: its flowers and its harvests
Strewed our footpaths and filled our granges;
My voice of April in May sang you the songs,
And I sang of them to you from June to Autumn Harvest.

I don't know – though haughty Art
Welcomed our first fruits with an indecisive smile –
They are like a kiss, a scent of thyme,
And a riff on the flute that novice fingers play,

And they deserve a bold and prompt reply,
For we both quivered with fine audacity
That evening when you crowned my brow with gay laurel
And pointed out the future, saying: take your place.

Dea

Quae laetificat juventutem meam...[2]

Imperious Poesy is my lover,
Very serious and learned too sometimes, like ladies
Of yesteryear, and sweet and tender in her blames;
Her proud step drags in heavy folds her sluggish dress
Where *Fleurs de Lys* shimmer brightly, like flames.

I know a valiant heart beneath her royal bosom,
Marmorean like the ancient Goddess;
I know the jealous love too great for my weakness
By which I merit what I merit, haughty and male,
Her heart and her love, and that She is my mistress.

The rhythm of her voice is my sole metric,
And her alternating pace, my nuanced rhyme;
My idea is what I have read in her thought,
Of course, and I have never dreamt of another America
Than to kiss the auburn-gold of her lowered head.

I have never wanted, in the active and holy life,
For anything but the hours that her gentleness gives my joy,
When longly I speak, when, so that she might believe me,
I am naïve as a simple child and without feint,
Loving the obscurity that her wing deploys.

And I will live in the shadow, at her feet, without sadness,
Having no ambition but to dream beside Her,
Without fear for me of an unfaithful future,
For I will have sung only for my sweet hostess,
A vague song of love in the shadow of her wing.

---

[2]*Quae... meam*: Latin for "who gives joy to my youthfulness." The relative pronoun in the original is masculine (*qui*) from the opening line of the prayer said at traditional mass in the Roman Catholic Church: "*Ad Deum qui laetificat juventutem meam.*" Here it is made to be feminine.

A Poem of the Sea

Tu septiformis munere. – ROMAN HYMN.

I
Mare vorax.

I came to you, Sea, as come your rivers,
Impetuous and strong, champing at the bit of their banks,
Your triumphant rivers in their declivitous courses,
Sweet and smiling rivers where you drink;

I came to drown my heart in your grey waves,
My heart and my proud thought of an insurgent;
Me whose adventurous dream has voyaged
Confident towards the acerbic glory of contempt;

O Sea, I have come to you, the Insatiable,
To the oblivious gulf and the immense tomb,
To submerge my pride in the abyss where retumbles
The ephemeral mist in the implacable mirage;

Sea, take my heart, with its dear and vain dreams,
And my futile love and its ambition,
Sea, in the passive forgetfulness of every vision,
I want to err amidst the mourning of your great pines;

For, by the sun-lit plain and in inebriety,
I have marched, radious with anticipated glory;
Sea of forgetfulnesses, be the end of my mad escape:
Behold a sun in distress that founders at large...

II
Mare ferox.

Under the infinite azure of glorious summers,
Flouting the blue vault like a rival,
You roll, in the pride of your immensities,

Majestic Sea, your triumphal swell;

And here, dazzled by superhuman dreams,
Is my heart, infatuated with unique privilege, casting
My inferior name to just tomorrows and giving
Rhythm to my laconic pride by your example.

Sure, it is good to have hammered out steel verse,
Sure, it is sweet to have lived the saintly poem,
And to have scorned the blames that ill become
The lips of the crowd, and to have stayed the same;

It is dignified to believe imperturbably
In the Ideal despised by those whom one acclaims,
And to have listened to her who refutes them
Having sung Her a chaste epithalamion.

Whether your name die, or whether it resound forever,
Whether it sink into oblivion, or haunt memories,
What do you care, O dreamer of blasphemous dreams
In the proud disdain of contempts and glories?

III
Mare tenax.

When rutilant and silent in the splendid west,
The glorious sun immerses itself in your golden waves,
I dream of the blue myth of beautiful Atlantis
That beneath your avid swell forever sleeps and dreams.

You keep the secret of smiling prairies
And of virgins culling laurel leaves and thyme,
The imperious rite of lingering theories,
And the aroma of the woods rising on mornings;

And me, who knows the locations of flowers and insomnia
Under the eternal day of an eternal spring,
When all supreme voluptuousness is infinite,

When in the embalmed air hover chanting wings;

Sweet land whence emerge grandiose rivers,
Strewn with nenuphars, cradling Halcyon nests,
Land where the Empyrean burns in apotheoses
Over the blinding light of beautiful acts;

I felt surging in me that dream of egoism
To keep, like you, the secret of my heart,
And not to give sight of the prism
To the imbecility of their mocking laughter.

IV

Mare salax.

"Listen, in the lascivious August night, listen:
It is like an extended sob of extenuated lovers;
The atmosphere throbs... Let's go, old heart, *en route*
To the appeasement of your impetuous instincts;

"Hear the voluptuous kiss of the waves,
Waves stifling the pebbles' laughter;
The night is weighty and languishes in vague desires,
It pales at the zenith of violet lightning flashes;

"Let's go, old heart, *en route* to your old delight,
That quivering of the strand evokes other nights;
On this swooning August evening nature is complicit
And the universe tipsy on fragrances and sounds..."

But your mad song was not cradling my soul
On that heavy summer evening, O libidinous Sea;
I had not on my heart the name of a laughing woman,
I was not opening my dream to your lubricity,

And, like Parsifal in the erotic garden
Among the flowers of evil and their temptations,
I did not dream, that evening, but on the authentic Masterwork

Wherein all our passions must converge.

V
Mare vecors.

The bloody purple embers die out, one by one,
Where the golden Dome, red in the light, collapses...
From the Day's debris and its ceremonies,
Clouds of smoke, black as ink, rise to the moon...

At large, in the night of waves and dreams,
A sinister rumbling bursts out, and, on the strands,
The howling winds mix with sobs;
O Sea, in your enormous fury you rise up!

Surge, break your fetters, devastate and destroy
This tottering world that devolves into rottenness,
Extirpate that dead wood and that barren tree,
Cleanse that teeming of unnatural beings!

Be the Deluge, be the extermination,
For Virtue does not exist, for Love is a kept woman,
For venal Glory is an ambition,
For the garden of the Dream is a dismal moor.

O, at least, until the day when this damned world
Submerges its leprosy in your vast bitterness,
Rise up on your beaches, unbridled Ocean,
And spit at it – with the bitter insult of your foam!

VI
Mare socors.

Sleep, Sea, insouciant and weary, what care you
For the arrogant whiteness of the cliffs? What care you
For the granites' reproach where your fury aborts?
That languid truce is better, in effect.

Sleep, beneath that sluggish midday of dream and inertia,
Impassible and smiling in your placidity:
In a tall pine's shadow, did I not sing for you
Of an old dream's sweetness that blossomed into poetry?

Did I or did I not approach you to find
The insouciance of being and the imbecility of laughter?
– What does the harvest matter? – I have thrown my sickle
Into the thistles along the path, and without knowing why.

… The laughter of your waves, soothing like rhymes,
And your fishing barques on too-blue horizons...
Here is the memory of a fabulous tale,
In unknown lands, beyond your abysses...

And your mirror that reflects of the past
Nothing but my hours of joy, serene and inactive...
And that white wake, of the Siren doubtless...
O Sea, let's sleep a while; this dream has made me weary.

VII
Mare livens.

The greens, burnt indigo, and pale azure
That your wave rolls in that impertinent splendor,
And the gold stars and the opal moon
That you swing in the night like a lantern,

You took them from the marvelous skies at dawn,
From dreams at midnight, from glories at sunset
To enhance the brilliance of your sonorous swells
And you seek the rocks' echo for their songs!

Do you not feel within you the opulence of being
Beautiful only by yourself, o Sea, and of being yourself?
Have you not your arcana that no eye may penetrate,
Like Space! and do you not, also, feel the terror?...

As for you, my heart, laughing in shame and recanting,
If their glory weighs on you with great ponderousness;
If, under the immensity of skies and geniuses,
Your mediocrity seems like a crime at times;

At least be proud, despite the hours of powerlessness;
Exult in being yourself, since you remain as you are –
You who have not, while rhythming a reminiscence,
Sought the plagiary that might have made me immortal!

Euphonies

I

"La belle dame sans merci."

Those were sweet hours,
O my lady of blonde roses,
When the swarm of dreams
Whirled in mad rings over the mosses,
And you said sweet things.

Those were dreamy kisses,
O my lady of blonde roses,
As if blossomed in other worlds;
And, under the rising moon,
I gathered dreamy kisses.

That was my radiant poem,
O my lady of blonde roses,
I would have drowned my very soul
Among the waves of your tresses:
And you no longer love that I love you.

II

On the old, flowering balcony, I sat my sadness
        Among your white roses,
And I heard what he said to you: "Dear countess,"
        And what you replied to him;
I heard the somniferous murmur of the bees
        Among your white roses;
You laughed, and I had to cover my ears;
        And the way you posed!
Ah! you did not see my soul agonizing,
        Among the white roses;
Did you not know that laughing was loathsome –
        How is it you dared to!

III
"Il voulut tout revoir..." – V.H.[3]

The quiet wave awakens and sings under our oars;
The whispering reeds recede; the old bridge
Comes alive with your laughter and responds...
Here is the wood of wild cherry trees we entered.

The plain is torporous like a lizard in the sun;
Vapors float in it like a somnolence;
And the grass is green, and the shadow sways above us...
Here is the spring that your ruby-red smile drank from.

The haystacks' shadow draws up conically to the moon
Which, from its heights, leaning over, looks down at
The day dying in the throes of sunset...
Here is the crepuscule and the importunate night.

The wave sings, wakening the dreamer,
The reeds in the summer night weep – it seems –
Echoes under the old bridge have a trembling voice...
Here is the smiling inn and the song of friends.

IV

The Dawn has virginal pudors, voices
That make the foolish dream of loving another,
In that solitude, alas! that once was ours
In days gone by, and all the past you see.

The Dawn has Your virginal pudors, Your voice.
Vibrant voice of old that no one else possessed;
But that very chaste and holy love that once was ours
Has departed from your dear soul, I see it.

With very slow steps, through the low bower where

---

[3]"Il voulut tout revoir...": French for "He wanted to see everything again" – Victor Hugo.

The duet of our voices sang our very first dream,
I walk, recounting that dream, it would seem to be another's.

O! let us die – what are they to me, the things I see,
And that solitude, alas! that once was ours,
And the Dawn, and your virginal pudor, and your voices!

V
"Oiseau bleu couleur du temps."[4]

Know you the forgetfulness
Of a vain, sweet dream,
Mocking bird
Of the forest?
The day fades,
Night rises,
And in my heart
The darkness has wept;

O sing to me
Your foolish range,
For I have slept
All the day;
The lax emotion
Where my soul was
Sobs among
The dying day...

Know you the song
Of her word
And of her voice,
You who repeat
In the sunset
Your frivolous air
As you did before
Under the midday suns?

---

[4]*Oiseau bleu couleur du temps*: French for "Blue Bird, blue as the sky" (*Green Fairy Book*). Originally, a line of verse from the tale written in French by the Countess d'Aulnoy (1650-1705).

O sing then
The melody
Of her love,
My foolish hope,
Among the golden hues
And the flames
Of the vain, sweet day
That dies this evening.

VI

"... Sola sub nocte..."

The words you spoke I retold them to the shade,
The glass you drank from I broke it in a rage;
Squatting in the sinister night on the strand
I hear the distant canon of a brig that sinks...

And what did my soul mean to you, sweet lady?
My ingenuous love, you must have smiled at it;
And then, in sum, was it up to me to tell it to you,
And did I need to hope you had seized my soul?

The beacon, in the west, alternates its colors;
The fatal *siren* ululates on the surface of the shoals;
But the glacial night is clear with pallors...

How was I to speak to you of roses and myrtles,
You whose changing eyes filled my heart with wonder,
You whose too sweet voice surprised my candor?

VII

To sleep and laugh with ease, a sleep: I ramble:
Let's sleep: the harm of loving, o heart, has ravaged you;
And I feel myself, this evening, so foolishly aged
That I believe myself the survivor of a vain world.

The night is formidable and sad till the end of days,
A memory that haunts fills the deserted darkness;
My regret is futile and my inert desire
No longer summons the hope of scuppered dreams;

Let's sleep: there's nothing left beneath the azure crepe
Where old joy was draped until the end of days:
Your wings which sacred desire opens and spreads

Fall again, your hope for love is almost impure...
I ramble on return from vain lassitudes,
Have we not dreamt of other beatitudes?

VIII
Rursus.[5]

Your heart weeps,
This evening in May,
Like a child;
Your heart weeps,
And it denies
Having loved
Like a child...

Your heart regrets,
This gentle evening,
Like a remorse;
Your heart regrets
Its dead dreams
And this hope,
Like a remorse...

Your heart hesitates
And is afraid to love
As at the beginning;
Your heart hesitates...

---

[5]*Rursus*: Latin for "backward."

And it is on the shore
Of that sea
As at the beginning...

Your heart is drunk
On the same wine
Without knowing it;
Your heart is drunk
This quiet evening,
Still in vain,
Without knowing it...

IX

Lætatus sum in his quæ dicta sunt mihi. – PSALMS 121.

The conscious dream that gives you my life
Is sad with the regret of future abandonments,
And the merry path, where age invites us
For one hour's stopover where we linger
In this joyous dream that gives you my life,
Leads us to the next crossroads of abandonments...
O the merry path where love invites us
And the languid stopover where we linger!...

This energetic dream is cowardly and crazy, in sum,
And that banal *always* is a liar in effect;
For superhuman fatality enjoins us that
The weft of our vows frays and comes undone,
And any pledge of love is weak and crazy, in sum;
For too well do I know the pledge I made,
And the fatal forgetfulness of tomorrow enjoins us,
And how this fragile bond comes undone...

But this idyllic dream is like the lull;
Your warm voice rocks me like an ocean;
And your words reach my sleeping soul
Like a vague song forgetful of the emptiness
Of that dream, of our love, and of its lull;

Let my soul drift far upon the ocean
And by your voice cradle itself asleep and dream;
For tomorrow it must weep for all this emptiness.

X
Plein air.[6]

Your head of hair, undone and loose,
Inundates and flows in the green grass
Like a clear rivulet sanded with gold
And, on your half-exposed breasts,
A vague ray of light dances or rests;
Distractedly, with half-open lips,
You laugh at the sky through the foliage...

O sweet vernal thing,
O young lady, o superb flower,
Let your royal nudity blossom
Amidst your sisters of the grass;
Your unconscious vanity
Glitters on a caustic lip
And gleams in your shock of hair.

Do not move: a violet shadow
Plays in the pink folds of your haunches;
Open your big, childish eyes
Where the pride of your white flesh grins...
O, has there even been in other Aprils
A similar feast under the branches?
And how vain is the palette!

XI

The broom have blossomed along sandy bank
Where the river last month brought its caprices,
And this slow July passed like a dream;

---

[6]*Plein air.* French for "open air."

The broom have blossomed along the dazzling bank...
Tell me that your kisses are naught but the signs,
That this slow July, which passed as if in a dream,
Was merely the prelude to supreme delights...

The sandy bank is blossoming with broom
That the river, laughing, bent last month;
The sand ripples in the hollows of abandoned beds,
The dazzling sand is blossoming with broom;
The breeze, cooled in the shade of old woods,
Drives the fine sand from its abandoned beds;
Things are not as they were that other time!...

XII
Stupeur épanouie. – V.H.[7]

Here is, for the span of one hour, a riverine dream.
The sands and grey willows, and the serene
Expanse of clear sky, and all the prairies
To the west where heifers graze
On flowers and sweet grass; and thus may you live,
Ignorant of whatever chance has led you here,
O laugher with the unconscious laugh, dreamer of the
Merry dream of April forests where a song of sap surges.

For the day is joyous and the river falls asleep:
One could cull the reflection of golden flowers there.

White flocs of cloud with grey fleeces vanish,
Scattered across the unconquered plains
In slow grazing flocks that a soft breeze,
Invisible shepherd of infinities, drives
So lightly that its passage barely brushes the water...

And the passivity of this hour is fecund.

_____

[7] *Stupeur épanouie*: French for "Radiant stupor." – Victor Hugo.

Rex

For Philibert Delorme.

He sits enthroned at the crossroads of worlds; by night,
Before the blinding parvis of marble and gold,
From the confines of space where Existence sleeps,
The couples come chanting – for death – heart upon heart;
And the altar bleeds and smokes before Him.

And, half-concealing a tender and crazed look,
He smiles at the songs of the beloved poets,
And blond Eve has made of her two swooning breasts
A pillow for his head, and the blamed dreams
Hum with the strange harmony of their flight.

All is burgundy – shame collides with pudor;
All is vibrant – the choral songs alternate, thus:
"Glory to God!" – In a nimbus of golden hues,
Here is Venus Imperatrix, and her throne too
Is tawny gold amid the marbles and their candor.

Here joy erupts into eternal laughter
That heaven's vault forever reverberates; here
Sensuous incense hovers, and all care
Dies in drunkenness; here the heart that one chose
Is abandoned: and this is the place of carnal triumphs.

The colonnade extends its marbles to the sea
By the mysterious flowering plains whence
Mounts an ecstatic inebriation; a mad wind
Rushes from the sea, and ringdoves nestled round virgins'
Necks preen their plumage where the clear wave

Sowed pearls; around the garlanded woods,
In the radiance of the insouciant throne,
The terrace with golden balustrades races beneath the skies
Of pale azure – and the choir chants – and all eyes

Blindly fix on the grim splendor of the dais.

Look! – on the horizon, until the darkness of evening,
Behold: an enormous blaze rolls forward,
The purple of its flame like a bloody flood tide
And its smoke, an atrocious froth; thus, beside
The rocks, the carnage of the surf runs black!

Sea of blood and mud and hatred; ocean
That rolls, scattered in the shadows, at the fatal whim of the waves,
The couples born of inexhaustible darkness, awakened
To the emptiness of human life and its sobs,
Toward eternal death and toward another emptiness.

Those of the golden terrace contemplate not
The morose infinity; and the hymn of their fearless
Soul chants, as far as the King's throne,
Among his choirs, the delights that their naïve heart
Blesses and believes to be eternal.

And the temple and the plain and the golden terrace
Resonate forever in continual hymn;
And forever and ever, Eros beams,
Arching his naked torso; and to the unknown end of days,
Couples will go, chanting, to their doom.

The Fruit

For Henri de Régnier.

Far from the ardent strand and the aridity
Where the river loses itself in the dunes' sand
We climbed back up the bank; an eternal summer
Burns in those places devoted to celestial rancors
Where the debris of an ancient city sleeps.

All day long, exalted in the dream of conquests,
Strong in the imperious desire of the Unknown,
We marched, and, sometimes, a mirage of crests
Perforated the silent and naked horizon:
We heard the poets' Lyre vibrate.

But the lingering hour cherished the skies; Infinity
Mounted the horizon in retrograde, in an insulting,
Inalterable expanse of the unified azure:
Despite the mocking contestation of each step
We marched towards the febrile goal of exile;

In the torrid, blinding light of the plain
That bristles with monoliths, we marched
Until evening, dreaming of the beneficent breath
Of a wood and the shade of palms; but no hope
Not even a floc of wool, appeared there.

Night refreshed; at dawn, as we marched
Along the sterile, gloomy bank, and along the path,
There appeared to the North, like fissures,
An undulation of hills; and the entire
Bank was imprinted with the seal of great lions.

Then we entered under lofty vaults
Pushing aside the entangled bramble bushes;
Between the gnarled trunks of walnut trees and oaks,
Colossal and older than the crumbled rocks,

The lianas weigh with their interlacing chains.

Farther on, the grass, tall like a forest,
With glimpses of azure behind it, lifts its golden tips
Where the sun shimmers like a golden wave;
And then comes the accustomed murmur of the waves,
And the river, now a stream, reappears;

From the strangely fecund plains of silt
Surges, as if haphazardly in all seasons,
The exuberant flora scattered across worlds;
And in the feral defoliation of florescences,
Our soul lingered among the soiled flowers.

We marched: before us, from the depths of a valley
To the boundless dome of timeless foliages,
In sprays both opaque emerald and crystal,
The source of the Euphrates shot up bubbling
With a harmonious sound of clear metal;

Decorated, like spring, with pink and white flowers,
Standing in the clearing, eternal and fatal,
And bent to the ground under the pride of its branches,
The Tree of Knowledge of Good and Evil
Stiffened its double trunk bulging like haunches.

At the base of the tree, with flowers on his knees,
Our soul said: Here is the fruit to slake yourself on;
And I took from him a fruit and found it to be sweet;
We enjoyed ourselves in the shade that the tree
Offered, and the voluptuousness of gods imbued us;

Insane hour! – puberty of illusion: our dreams
Came alive at the sole wishes of our creative desires,
But, joy once ecstasiated, that you might find completion,
The Tree of Evil amassed on us its flowers,
And centuries passed before us like brief hours...

Hunger came upon us thus, like a death;

The avenging angel of Adam and Eve's sweet sin,
In the immobility of a golden simulacrum,
Holds the flame of its Sword in a clenched fist,

And Eden appears, over there, like a décor!...

Carmen Perpetuum

Mixtam te varia laudavi saepe figura. – ÉLÉGIE LATINE.

PRELUDE

The imperial Aurora and its purple have passed;
Behold the wood's song and the plain's rumor
And spring mixing its sounds and its exhalations
With my soul, drunk on love, smitten with the past.

The grass is joyous and around the river that wends
Majestic and slow in lost horizons
Quiet murmurs arise, as were heard
Before last winter, and before my life began...

Just as on this prestigious April morning,
Inhaling the voluptuousness of superhuman Things,
I follow, unconscious, the path where you lead my being
Toward an end unknown to both of us;

Thus did I drink love from your diverse lips
Since the time of first dawn and the start of eternity;
And until that April when your nudity laughed
I held out a crater[8] for the kisses that you pour;

Our forgotten vows are like a remorse to me,
I have followed the mysterious echoes of your laughter;
And in my astonished eyes wherein you see yourself
The lost brilliance of dead suns is reflected.

I

I erred in a nameless Land, among flowers,
Dreamless, without a past, joyous with a strange joy;

---

[8]crater: in ancient Greece or Rome, a bowl or vase shaped like an amphora.

Childlike and laughing for the sounds and colors,
In my virginal virility of an archangel.

Lascivious and blonde in the grass, green with blue reflections,
You slept at my feet in fatal expectation;
And the conspiring rose, shedding a petal,
Made your lips spread into a smile that was mellow...

You lay at my feet, cheerful and blushing,
In your passivity of a lover, you lay,
And you understood, at first, the Word that I spake;
And the kiss was long, and strong was the embrace.

II

The vertiginous wave swept the hills away
And tracked that human prey to the side of the mountain;
With the mocking cries of demons, the winds
Sullied your nudity with saline smudges;

Amidst the resounding crumbling of the summits
Like a supreme defiance before a devastating God,
The colossal rock in all its height
Stood unshakeable in the distance over the abysses...

The horror of near nothingness distracted your voice
In blasphemies – tender song of our impure love –
My shivering lips forgot the sure fruit
Where we had bitten the forgetfulness of vain problems;

But, drowning your loud cries and my man's insult,
Heaven's howling filled the immensity:
On the block, impassive in its enormity,
The entire gulf surged, a dreadful dome!

You smiled at me then, frantic, of terror weary,
And as the embrace stirred our blasé appetites,
That dying was merely, for our interlaced bodies,

The devourment of their carnal ecstasy.

III

Naïvely lubricious, with an eye out for an old faun,
You exited, beaming nymph whom the storm arouses,
In pursuit of vernal love that the brutal embrace
And the aphonic kiss appeases in a rage.

On seeing you, I picked up my Lydian flute,
So that, to hear me and perhaps to see me,
And believing yourself hidden in the shade of a large beech tree,
You tiptoed near me, curious, and already mine.

O how you laughed, dryad, then when, taken,
You had forgotten the old faun and the footpath;
The azure, seeing you fall into the caressing grasses,
Smiled through the laburnum branches.

A breeze fragrant with thyme from the pasturage
Rose up – hour of idyllic shamelessness –
But we did not notice the oblique shadow lengthening,
And we did not hear the storm troating in the distance.

IV

In the freshness of an aromatic October evening,
In the land of sluggish and voluptuous love,
Drinking to drunkenness, O blonde woman, the troubling
Aroma that that Attic crepuscule exhaled,

I dreamt of the apparatus of all your pallors,
I dreamt, crouching in the shadow and in expectation,
And, filled with a great desire for your tempting whiteness,
I garlanded your threshold with white flowers...

Surprised by a sob borne to you on the breeze,

Leaning out in the starry night, you saw me;
And, happy to see me caught off guard,
Amidst my white flowers, you said: Open the door!

V
Fontanalia.
(The feast of fountains.)

You suspended garlands from the branches,
Around a venerated basin dear to naiades;
You looked at yourself sometimes, laughing at the eyes
You made... an indiscreet stone effaced

That coquettish laugh from the undulating mirror;
And you were sixteen on the calends of May...
It is the mirage of your too-loved laughter
That earned you, that day, my naïve request;

I brought you, a spouse, before the lares of the hearth;
You were my high-strung and haughty Egeria,
For that laughter emerged from the antique fountain
Where I plunged my heart, that day, to drown it.

VI
"La belle Aude."

The annoying languor of slowly-playing violincellos
Reiterates that our hope for love is infantile;
The quiet hautboy modulates a faraway regret;
A sound with large wings quivers in the orchestra;

The very shrill flute with Satanic stridencies
Mocks an intermittent sob that the horn produces:
Then lo and behold, is it not, the heroic décor
Of roaring mountain streams and titanic rocks;

Behold the shock of irons and cries of carnage,

Rage clutching at the sides of sobbing rocks,
The mortal fall and, around the white peaks,
The prodigious flight of vultures plunges and swims...

And, over there, on the Rhone, a funeral chant,
Immense and sad chant that weeps for a people in mourning;
And blood roses on the double coffin;
And Durandal with the glory of battles!

VII

The aureoled queen with the effaced smile,
In her stellular robe of white ermine,
And her pomp on days of High Mass has passed,
With her gentle female gaze, which dominates...

Then, beneath the rumbling of unleashed organs
Where the glorious flight of hymns wed,
My heart grew exasperated in a damned dream
Among the hallelujahs of Palm Sunday:

Head high, braving the brilliance of the monstrance
And that people, bent over, whom fear prostrates,
With a long sob of loving you hopelessly,
I prayed to you, on both knees, like a Saint.

VIII

We were not shepherds, at the time of *pastorals*,
In the days of my epic Brittany when you loved me;
And I departed for distant fishing grounds.

In the long sobs of winds mixing with the cry of masts
I had harmonized some male reveries
Full of aromas imbibed under foreign climates.

O the return, hope cradled by my sluggish nights!

And your image, like a beacon in the orient;
So much so that I espied shimmering stars;

At last, the arduous coast in smiling sunlight;
Sinister and troubling apprehensions;
Then, interlaced joy and the fond kiss.

And we believed, in times of *philosophy*,
In the days of my ever orthodox Brittany,
Obstinately mystical and whose soul blindly

Trusts in the Christ of calmed oceans,
Whose immense heart of granite builds a Temple
Where the sea roars and the sky is filled with stars.

We believed in a love that would last a lifetime,
Ignorant moreover of shameless capriciousness,
Innocent of the desires of satisfied shame;

We did not understand the mockers' laughter;
We dreamt, beyond a tooth-and-nail existence,
Of a Sky where the best draw near Christ.

IX

Would I have found love anyways? – the day slumbers
In the occident, come back: did I not lead you
Wither the suave perfume of a dead dream lingers,
O Berthe, o my Gretchen, o my sweet Renée?

… Your wide eyes, and ingenuous pigtails, and your voice,
Merry and musical, in naïve replies,
And your celestial candor when you explain to me
The fabulous wherefores of the things you see...

Unique hour of thoughtless and chaste love,
The burning crepuscule of a radiant summer; –
O the candid and tender Idyll that it was;

Despite that other ill-starred evening that occurred.

Seated on your knees in the shade where your shape
Was drowned, I listened to your voice, as if in ecstasy:
Every naïve contour seemed like a phrase to me;
The unexpected and crazy words that the spring

Breeze brought me from your mischievous lips
Appeared to ripple around your body;
For me, colors and sounds became confused then
In the intoxication of loving a childlike woman...

The Lady Who Wove

"Kissing her hair..." – ALGERNON CHARLES SWINBURNE.

Springlike, in the dream's eternal dawn
And sitting in the aurora, She weaves while dreaming
Of things She knows, and smiles; and, before
Her, in her agile hands, the laborious shuttle
Runs without stopping, and the gentle April
Breeze tousles her hair which She lifts
And throws over her shoulder; and, raising
Her head, hums a tune She does not complete...

In the shade She appears as if framed in gold:
Behind her the azure and the plains that a river
Irrigates; and above her head, a branch of oleander
Spreads its flowers against the clear blue sky; – and the effort
Of her loom, like a monotonous and morose song,
Moans very softly; – One would envy the fate
Of the man who kissed the hand that she lets fall
Negligently, sometimes, weary from the effort...

But me, seeing her laugh while doubtless recalling
Some sweet bygone day of her joy, one May evening,
I imagined that others, perhaps, for having loved
Her laugh, took the slow road again,
Sad with a memory and their heart hankering
After a sweetmeat that no lips taste with impunity;
For in its crazy thirst my mouth named her
While invoking her: O Queen, o blonde Queen, hear me out!

Then, turning her gentle, loving gaze on me,
She said: Child, your soul is marvelous
And its desire is puerile; me, the eternal old
Lady for whom the aurora, one vain day
That never comes, is golden; my destiny:
Carder of the Work I weave and unweave, to and fro,
On the loom; what difference is it to me, being derisive

And neglectful of my body, your virginal love?

Then, seeing me cry like a child she had wounded,
She smiled and said: Take a skein then and recount
For me that great love of yours, new dreamer
Of the old dream of every other man; your feebleness
Is confident and youthful, and its candor earns you
A place at my feet; sit, dream, and sing and let
Your foolish soul go, and, holding the purple skein,
Search my clear eyes for that unique intoxication.

And I was exhausted then like a person with a fever,
Listening to that Lady's scoffing voice;
But, before Her seated, I felt a voracious fire
That consumed my life and, freed
Of all fear, I sang the epithalamion
Of aggrieved love, in a slow and sad rhythm,
So that, leaning towards me, the gentle Lady
Touched me with a kiss that nothing has weaned.

And as the skein of purple thread, that her agile hand
Unwound, filled the shuttle, while singing
My dream, I braided her hair; and the rhythm
Of my auroral and candid song so charmed
Her heart by its voluptuousness that, hearing me,
The Lady forgot herself and her slow empty gaze
Wandered along the river and the plain; and, meanwhile,
Her white hand shivered under my avid kisses.

And turning her long, misty gaze towards me,
In a very soft voice, She said: "Stay, page,
And sing like that, the dream of another age;
I permit you to live here... But look, that wheat
Seems like gold over there..." And in that sweet
Language I heard a great, hidden wish for love,
And then came the tears, streaming down her cheeks,
And her blue eyes glistened like a starry sky.

Mystical Hour

In memoriam C. G.

I

"Jejuna Corda." – BOOK OF HOURS.

The roses along the way evoke other roses;
Imperious April evokes another Love;
That future, joyous hope, that you propose,
Recalls from the past the shadow of another day;
The roses along the way evoke other roses.

The virginal catafalque – o white roses! –
The candles in the night of mourning; the heavy step
Of men; the lumbering organ – as of our Sundays
Formerly –; and the indifferent crowd around
The virginal catafalque with the white roses.

Those days are dead; your life, setting off at dawn,
Would founder before the stunned aurora where I go,
Ambitious dreamer of improprietous victory
And defying the memory of bad days:
Those days are dead; the aurora has repressed that dawn.

Tell me, you who dreamt of the archangel's harp,
On that evening of intimate conversation, whether the God
Of former days had taken you amidst the harmonious
Phalanx of his choirs, and tell of the Very Holy
Place where your voice of an archangel sings to his Christ...

Of course, and you know Rhythms and Dreams
And some unappeased Love of sister souls;
And you take pity on our art and its beloved untruths,
And the dear banality of hearts;
And you know Love, Rhythms, and Dreams.

O Sweet deceased, o feverish child, dead with the drunkenness

That sanguineous Wine gives elect hearts; and we,
Despite that at the crossroads of all roads stands
The prestigious cross that one kneels down to kiss, –
We have preferred Life to that drunkenness.

Crazy with emancipated desires and young love
For the universe conquered by our timorous vows,
We marched, showering with hope the fasting
Of hearts; and we proceeded to unknown goals
In drunken joy and the feverishness of fasting.

And even though we went among white roses,
Willy-nilly along the green path, that fine April day,
The memory struck me of the hillock where you repose
Asleep in the hope of a puerile dream;
The roses along the way evoking other roses...

So much so that, in the evening that comes, my soul is sad
Vaguely, without regret, if it isn't with a hope
And that my gentle and impetuous heart might resist
The promises of a loving shadow and, in the evening
That comes very slowly over us, my soul is sad.

II
Ite, missa est. – Divine office.

O futile player of the lyre, evoke a shadow;
For your soul would weep for joy on the evening of grace,
Before that long road that your ruin encumbers.

Your tongue is tied now, unable to pray;
The hour is funereal; it is in vain that your eye scours
The dark immensity of the Occident without a trace.

Your soul savors nothing that is sullied
By the daily disavowal of each prior evening.
Ennui gnaws at your heart like bitter rust.

Stop dreading that your will might awaken
From the drowsiness that your disdain imposes
And that, sometimes, your mind itself wonders at.

Stop disdaining to quit the indefectible pose
By which the proud allure of your life stiffens,
O you, whose pity extends over everything.

For the staying pride of the dream that defies
Sacred love to the point of desiring to vanquish it,
Teaches you the disdain that severs and deifies

Your skeptical reasoning which nothing could convince.

*

Yet it would have sufficed from that monitory mourning
To revive in you the magical credence
And bend your knees before the Holy Ciborium.

Pick up your lyre again and rhythm anew the supplication
Of a humiliated song that laments and glorifies,
From the threshold, the holy Lamb of tragic Mass.

Say: "Christ, my heart is weary and my barque wanders
Where the storm wills it, towards eternal death;
Of the feast of the flesh my soul is satisfied."

Say again: "Christ God, is my soul not worthy
Of one drop of the True Blood that a priest pours,
And have you no concern for my immortal soul?"

Get drunk on the incense tumbling in an avalanche
From choir to parvis where you pray in the shadows,
And behold, suddenly, your soul is all white!

To the golden ciborium studded with precious stones,
Wherein the vivifying Bread lies, advance and eat:
For Christ will not lose Those he has fed.

Feel the angel reawakening at the bottom of your abject being,
Glimpse, for one instant, the Heaven for which wisemen
Have disdained the earth and the love of its filth;

And Voices will speak ecstatic messages to you...

*

O vision of an evening and the royal escort
Of archangels, players of the harp, and of one hundred virgins...
But the sky of the elect has closed its door again;

In the silver dawn, the slow death of candles...
And the banality of things and of men,
The sewer wherein you are immersed forever, poor heart.

Break your crucifix, cast the atoms of the futile Ideal
To the winds and follow the slow crowd;
For we do not know even what we are.

Your fine and valiant faith is quite dead now, go;
Your eternal barque brails its double sail;
In the passive stagnation of an expectation,

And above you the firmament slowly recedes;
It is the grievous hour when the soul, regret without hope
And night without star, drapes itself in darkness,

And it is the obscurity that weighs like a blame.

III
Sile!

The penumbra languishes on Pindus' Peaks;
A silent black lake in the crux of a valley, – and it is night;
The axis of heaven rotates the fires of India round us.

Throw down your bow, whistle after your bloodhound that pursues
Its vain chase into the dark of night – the darkness is dismal;
Sit down near the water that gurgles, your body is tired.

The moon lifts its double horns in the east;
Respite falls from on high on the audacious dream;
Behold the mosses of a boundary stone for you to lean on.

Fix your sight on a star, know the vertigo of the heavens;
Dissolve yourself into Space like smoke,
And, in the voluptuousness of Nothingness, close your eyes.

It sings now with voices under the leafy boughs,
A light wind rustles in the grass where you lie!
What were you doing pursuing frenetic renown?

It is beneath *you* – despite its reddened horizons,
Despite the dawn and the sea, this world is a bauble;
And art is not worth the trouble – o rhythm – and you bawl.

Prayer is absurd the moment you dare to say it;
Are you not ashamed also of your God who was weeping?
The time for Christ and the apotheosis is long past.

What naïve fatuity deluded you
With a childish hope and an impossible fantasy,
Promising glory to your frightened dream?

Turn your eyes longly again on the impassive sky –:
The only Glory is to be Infinite!
Are you sure you would not want an accessible glory?

Abdicate being king, – would you recognize him, banished –
Knowing that the only worthwhile thing is tilting your will
In daily combat against whomever pride whinnies at.

Be silent; stop dreaming of the splendor that intoxicates you:
That impotent joy is the worst – an hour has flown by –
What would you expect, you who disdain living...

The great starry sky revolves in the night.

Epilogue

Sunset and dawn spill the feral blood of days;
The acrid sea projects its scum that the wind carries
To fresh-water rivers; and we, who drank
The air of grassy plains and bare peaks,
Drunk on you, Wine of Being that consumes the soul,
We proceed to Death, which nothing escapes:

At the old road's edges that your April enflowers,
Earth, o sterile Mother with the hard chest,
Are not darkness of oaks, sheen of prairies,
And the horizon propitious to the virile wish?
For passionate Life widens its portal,
And Heaven's eternal smile is puerile.

As others before us have gone, and, despite the Shadow
Where, beyond our joyous days, the route vanishes,
As carefree as the goat that grazes,
We will go, slowly, without keeping count,
Until that fatal evening of torments and doubt,
Until the funereal night, and until the Shadow...

Life is long; Art fills its golden cup;
Hope bubbles up in pure gold at the crater's edge!
Merry Youth shows a sure path
To Peaks where a blinding flight of large swans goes;
And we go, drunk on the azure;
Beneath our feet the teeming of a people sleeps.

Already, for our astounded gazes, the plains
Lie in matutinal splendor and joy
Under the tender sky that a pale haze drowns
In its dream; and around us a sound of breaths
Rises among the branches and the horizon outspreads
The vaporous immensity of the distant plains;

The day we dreamt of, born on that morning

Of pink gold, vibrates and sings: our wishes are fulfilled.
Our new and adolescent soul has lapses of memory
That make yesterday's shame resemble distant illusions;
And the zephyr carries, in its weakened rhythms,
The mysterious echo of some other morning...

Rise, sing! now is the hour for great things;
Your plectrum is made of gold; raise your imperious head
While opening your princely coat; for the cheerful
Goddess Hebe has told you: Give God my offerings.
The holy viaticum of the pious stage
Has nourished your beautiful soul for great things;

The orient expands, and there, as far into the infinite,
Which the joyful escape of pallors unveils,
An ocean unfolds and one hears the crash
Of its waves, cheerful blue reflections of blessed sky...
– O, our soul comes towards you avid for good fortune,
Skies, Ocean, double azure of the Infinite!

Our life's blood is generous in boldness,
The path to the top is easy for those who risk it;
And in the glorious hymn of some apotheosis
The royal retinue of the Thracian pastor advances:
Before him, shedding leaves of myrtle and rose,
The virgins proceed, shining with youthful grace;

Not one of the strings of the Orphic Lyre
Is busted; the quiet song of Virgins can still be heard;
Nothing has changed of the imperishable décor:
For sempiternal Spring dies and is reborn;
Despite that at the foothills the multitude sleeps
And the holy Temple grieves, profaned...

Other Books by the Publisher

Fanchette's Pretty Little Foot by Restif de La Bretonne

Je M'Accuse... by Léon Bloy

My Hospitals & My Prisons by Paul Verlaine

Salvation Through the Jews by Léon Bloy

Words of a Demolitions Contractor by Léon Bloy

Cellulely by Paul Verlaine

Ecclesiastical Laurels by Jacques Rochette de la Morlière

Flowers of Bitumen by Émile Goudeau

Songs for Her & Odes in Her Honor by Paul Verlaine

On Huysmans' Tomb by Léon Bloy

Ten Years a Bohemian by Émile Goudeau

The Soul of Napoleon by Léon Bloy

Blood of the Poor by Léon Bloy

Theresa the Philosopher & The Carmelite Extern Nun by Marquis d'Argens & Anne-Gabriel Meusnier de Querlon

A Platonic Love by Paul Alexis

Two Novellas: Francine Cloarec's Funeral and Benjamin Rozes by Léon Hennique

The Revealer of the Globe: Christopher Columbus & His Future Beatification (Part One) by Léon Bloy

Joan of Arc and Germany by Léon Bloy

Héloïse Pajadou's Calvary by Lucien Descaves

An Immodest Proposal by Dr. Helmut Schleppend

The Pornographer by Restif de La Bretonne

Style (Theory and History) by Ernest Hello

On the Threshold of the Apocalypse: 1913-1915 by Léon Bloy

She Who Weeps (Our Lady of La Salette) by Léon Bloy

The Sylph by Claude Prosper Jolyot de Crébillon (*fils*)

School of Woman by Nicolas Chorier

Voyage in France by a Frenchman by Paul Verlaine

Ourigan, Oregon by William Clark, Richard Robinson, and anonymous

Drowning by Yu Dafu

www.ingramcontent.com/pod-product-compliance
Lightning Source LLC
Chambersburg PA
CBHW031257120626
46545CB00007B/2859